Letters to my GrandSon

with Love,

Made in the USA
Las Vegas, NV
13 September 2023

77514928R00079